PARENTING TO PREVENT AND REVERSE PROBLEM BEHAVIORS

How To Instill

Empathy, Values, Morals,
Ethics, Responsibility and Self-Esteem

C.E. Luradel

Into Me I See
Publishing

Printing, 2018

ISBN 978-0-9990597-0-8 (Paperback)
ISBN 978-0-9990597-1-5 (eBook)

Printed in the United States of America.

Publisher: Into Me I See Publishing
Box 323, Tualatin, OR 97062-9361

intomeiseepublish@gmail.com

THIS BOOK IS DEDICATION TO

All the World's Children and Parents
I hope this book gives you new Hope, Direction, and Tools for learning
how to do life & living.

All my Children ... M.D.J.T.
Thank you for teaching me what does and doesn't work in Parenting

This Parenting Manual has been designed for parents and children to participate as a family. The manual lays out in detail how to instill 40 character-building behaviors into your child that ensure they will have a life of meaning and purpose. The spacious 8 x 11 size comfortably allows this manual to lay open for hands-free viewing, enabling families to clarify and discuss all aspects listed. Included are a variety of areas where family members can write comments or even lay out specific directions, customizing behaviors that are just the right touch for your family. The first portion of the manual is directed mainly toward the parent, while the second portion is intended as a reference guide for children to learn the full particulars of each desired behavior. These behaviors will be viewed almost on a daily basis and the manual will become well-worn through consistent researching of each listed behavior.

Table of Contents

1

WHY I WROTE THIS BOOK

◦

On April 1st, an 18 yr old woman and a 23 yr old man welcomed their second son into the world. Both parents love this child very much and wanted the best the world had to offer for him. These young parents did what they had learned about parenting from their parents, who learned from their parents and all the many generations before them on how to raise a child. All the psychology experts and medical doctors in childrearing also made it clear how it was all to be done.

Feed the newborn by a set schedule and do not give into them when they cry demanding more. Feed them rice cereal at two weeks old so they will sleep through the night. Do not pick them up when they cry or you'll spoil them. The child was told what he was doing wrong and he was punished with negative consequences, such as taking away privileges, being given extra duties around the house, or grounded for being bad.

And worst of all, his parents told their son he was responsible for what they thought, felt, said, or did. They would say things like: you made me feel ashamed of you, you made me angry, and you are a disappointment to our family and me. They told him they worried that he wouldn't amount to much in life, as his schoolteacher said he wasn't learning because he didn't want to do the work. When he continued to wet the bed at night at 10 yrs old, the doctor said he was lazy and just didn't want to get up and walk to the restroom. The parents believed the doctor because, after all, he was a doctor who saw hundreds of children in his practice. So the parents told their boy he was lazy and they were mad that he was. They warned him that, if he didn't stop wetting the bed, they would make him wear diapers.

These two parents continued to obey the parenting rules laid out and taught to them, even though the rule was that children need to be seen, but not heard. They told their son to suck it up and be a man when he cried. They told him he was weak in an attempt to make him strong, saying "Don't cry or I'll give you something to cry about". They told him he isn't trying or applying himself when he doesn't learn. They told him he couldn't do something, to make him want to do that thing. They would tell him where everything he did is wrong and ignored the correct areas, in an effort to make him want to do it perfectly correct.

Even though the parents found out that all the psychology experts, medical doctors and even teachers were wrong, no one could undo the damage that had already been done. They found out that their son had a learning disability, that his brain wouldn't wake him up at night when his bladder was full, and that it was really okay for him to cry. The parents realized that their son didn't make them feel all those emotions, such as sadness, shame, anger and disappointment – rather; they were echoing what their parents had said to them while they were growing up.

All those dehumanizing damaging rules that were almost impossible to carry out, because it made the young mother cry to treat her children that way and it just felt all wrong. She just wanted to hold him in her arms, tell him it would be alright and that they would find a way to make it work. She was told that, if she loved her child and wanted to be a good parent, she would take her child in hand and train him right.

When he was little and cried in his crib, she would go outside away from the pain of not being able to hold him. Outside she would talk to the other mothers in the neighborhood who were doing the same thing with their children. She wasn't going to think of her need to hold him, or any of her own needs and hurt her child by over-cuddling him. She would let him grow into a strong man.

In time, this young boy became angry and deeply depressed. He had zero self-esteem and, as a teenager, he turned to drugs to escape the voices in his head, reminding him of how worthless he was, and that he couldn't do anything right. Of how much pain and embarrassment he was causing to those who loved him.

He had a multitude of friend relationships that decayed and ended. He had a marriage that deteriorated and ended. He had jobs that crumbled and ended. He had sobriety for short periods of time only to relapse again and again. Every time he couldn't make life work, society let him know his value and how he was a huge failure as a human being. The voices that echoed in his mind, telling him he was worthless, also continued in his outside world on a daily basis.

One night he called a counselor woman he knew and said, "I just can't get how to do life. No matter how hard I try, I just don't get it, and all I do is keep hurting my parents because I can't get it. Now they won't ever have to hurt again because of me." Those were his last words; he ended the voices in his head by taking his own life.

There is no stronger love in this world than that of a parent for their child. Losing their son brought his parents to their knees. They tried to do everything they thought was the best for their child and are still lost on how everything went so terribly wrong.

We, as a human society, are programmed to notice all the errors, mistakes, inaccuracies, blunders, goofs, wrongs, laziness, inaptitude, etc., that others do or don't do in life and living, without valuing the effort, fails, trying, or any of the other positives. We, as a society, think that we are duty bound to tell them and everyone else how not to do anything or everything. We as a society need to turn this pattern of destructive behavior around.

WORDS

Have the Ability

to

Empower or Destroy

Choose Them Wisely

C.E. Luradel

In the end, it was the words that were said that shred him to pieces. Words shred a person's soul... so choose them wisely.

Why am I writing this Parenting Manual? Because I do not want ANY more children raised with these types of destructive rules ever again. I do not want to save one child from the words that shred; I want to save them ALL.

You can't just point out what not to do. You have to guide a child, show them the way it's done and together find what works, and always be available for support and guidance

Without its feathers a bird cannot fly. Give your child the gift of feathers that represent all the Values & Principles of how to do life – Let Go –then, stand back and watch them use those feathers to FLY. All on their own.

———

As a parent of four children, I've made more than my share of mistakes. I listened to what people and professionals were telling me on how to raise children. Even now, years later, I see many misguided ideas being passed onto parents today.

It wasn't until I became a behavioral health counselor working with hospitals, treatment centers, and having a private practice that I observed the family's dynamics and the behaviors of troubled teenagers. I learned the most effective method for transforming these teenagers was a system of Earn All.

If the teenager wanted something during their time in the treatment center, they had to earn it. A teenager who wanted a ten-minute telephone call to home had to earn that item by doing assigned tasks, such as make their bed every morning, take showers, comb their hair, not cuss for a certain amount of days, not hitting or fighting, write out a personal self-assessment of who they are, including weakness and strengths and share it with others in a group meeting.

These teenagers were not entitled to anything, and everything was viewed as a privilege to be earned. Most fought this new system. Being locked up was the worst thing that ever happened, and they would fixate on how their life would be once they could just get out of this place.

I witnessed the personalities of these teens transform dramatically under the conditions of Earn All. After a short time, they reflected new attitudes, a positive self-worth, confidence, and thinking they could ... and would ... conquer their life's dreams.

At the end of their treatment stay, the majority didn't want to leave. They had bonded with the other teens more closely than they ever had previously in life. All the teenagers supported each other and cheered for one another's accomplishments and gave unconditional understanding and support when they didn't do well. For some, it was the first time in their life they felt they were unconditionally heard, trusted, loved, valued, and came to believe they had purpose.

When the teenagers returned home to a family system that continued in the same dysfunctional ways, unfortunately most of these teenagers reverted to their old ways. Four to six weeks was not enough time to make these new behavior changes permanent.

I realized what we, as health care providers, wanted to teach these teenagers came from them Earning it. That's when it hit me: What are the most important things in life I wanted my children to learn? I took all those things and incorporated them into this book. There is magic in the behaviors listed, custom developed for learning how to do life in a healthy functional way.

I approached the writing of this book with great excitement as, in my heart, I've always wanted to help children and families. This method is a proven and effective answer to instilling healthy positive behaviors to our children, which builds a strong family unit and a positive life.

This book is dedicated to all Families and Children of the world, who in my heart, I've always wanted to help. It's my gift to you.

Children Are The Future

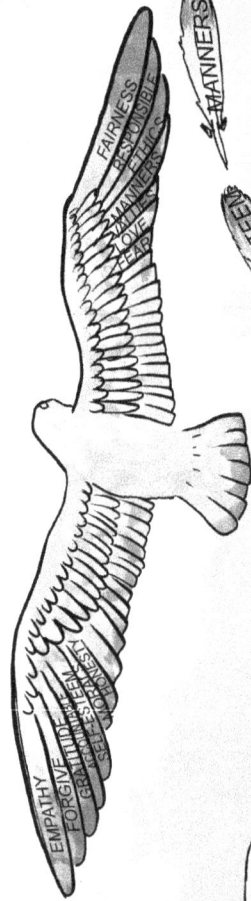

Give Them Feathers

LET GO

Watch Them Fly

VALUES
MORALS
FORGIVE
RESPONSIBILITY
GRATITUDE
LOVE
MANNERS
HONESTY
SELF-ESTEEM
ACCOUNTABLE
FAIRNESS
FEAR

EMPATHY
FORGIVENESS
GRATITUDE
SELF-WORTH
FAIRNESS
RESPONSIBLE
ETHICS
MANNERS
RESPECT
LOVE
FEAR

2

WHAT IS A PARENT

❧

A Parent is a Teacher to their Child of How To Do Life in All Aspects.

A parent teaches their child:

- How to comb their hair

- How to be kind

- How to be accountable

- How to apologize

- How to give & receive compliments

- How to honor commitments

13

- How to see beauty in all things
- How to work for what they want in life
- How to achieve a goal
- How to treat people with kindness
- How to eat healthy foods
- How to be respectful
- How to color inside & outside the lines
- How to laugh
- How to brush their teeth
- How to button their shirt
- How to pee in a toilet
- How to tie their shoes
- How to be gentle
- How to be fallible
- How to be special & humble at the same time
- How to play ball
- How to be a team player
- How to be compassionate
- How to see & feel unconditional love
- How to be moral
- How to have integrity
- How to do relationships

The list of what a parent teaches their child is virtually endless.

A baby's first act after being born is to cry. They cry when they're hungry, physically uncomfortable, or tired. The parent's goal is to figure out what this crying baby desires and provide it to end the crying of the unhappy baby. The baby learns crying brings a person who will give them what they want.

Now the stage is set, and the pattern of behaviors are established by both baby and parent. Both have now learned a crying baby means needs and/or wants are to be met. This urge is as strong for the parent as it is for the baby.

The problem arises when the child becomes verbal and can say they are hungry, physically uncomfortable, or tired, but still cries for all their needs and wants to be met. Because it is an established routine, the parent continues to provide whatever the crying child wants. A parent may say no to the child's demands, and the child will only escalate their crying, even reaching tantrum levels. Now comes the wisdom to know when, where, and how to change this pattern of behaviors.

Maybe the child's tantrum is being acted out in public where the embarrassment and shame of such a behavior makes it so much harder to handle. Perhaps, it's just a parent's caring heart that can't handle seeing their child suffer. Whatever the reason, often parents will give in to the child's demands, because they want the crying, screaming, and tantrums to end. The problem is, every time a parent gives the child what he is demanding, it reinforces that behavior in the mind of the child.

The child thinks, "cry, scream, stomp, and I get what I want." When a parent gives in to the child's demands, it's for their own peace of mind, not for the child. The parent wants the situation to go away and the happy smiling child to return. The crying child emotionally stresses the parent, because they have been mentally, psychologically, and emotionally programmed to provide for that child's every want and need. The parent's motto is to make their child happy and smiling at all costs.

You hear parents say, "I just want my child to be happy" or "It feels so good when I give him something and get to see that big happy smile on his face." That is not what makes a child happy.

A child that feels they are entitled to whatever they want will not have a happy functional life ahead of them. What they have learned is the world revolves around them, and they will lack the capacity to feel empathy for the needs of others. This child was not born with entitlement issues; they learned it through this behavior.

There are healthier and more functional ways a parent can teach their child how to obtain real happiness. Happy can come from achieving a goal, learning something new, helping others, noticing beauty in our world, or from walking through a fear. A child wanting something is motivation inside of them to obtain that thing they so desire. It's not for a parent to provide it to them, simply because they want it. That teaches nothing that would be productive in life. It only reinforces manipulative behaviors and a sense of entitlement.

Watch animals with their young. Initially, the mother is devoted to her young, never leaving their side and providing for their every need and safety. Gradually, as her young grow older, gaining more skills, the mother is less attentive, but still overseeing their every move. As the offspring learns and their abilities develop, they are also expected to do more for themselves on their own. The mother shows them how and then walks away, observing their ability to repeat what they've been shown.

The mother teaches their children how to do life, how to shelter themselves from weather, what to eat and how to find food on their own, how to interact with species of their own kind and species of other kinds, what to do and not do to live and survive.

An example scenario would be: When a child is learning how to walk, a parent will walk along holding both the child's hands, so they don't fall. If the parent doesn't let go at some point, the child will never learn balance, nor master the ability to walk unassisted. As time passes, the child will become fearful of walking without the aid of his parent's hands holding him. The child will have developed no confidence in their ability to walk alone. The parents have expressed an unspoken message to their child that they think they cannot do it on their own. So, they never let go of their hand, and the child never learns how to run free and will now fear the unknown.

Just like the letter A is the first letter of the 26 letters of the alphabet to be learned, after a child learns all 26 letters, there comes the combining of the letters to make a word... and each word has a meaning. Each step needs to be learned before going forward to the next. Then, in time and before you know it, they are writing the next great novel. After your child has learned to walk, by falling down hundreds of times, they've acquire the gift of confidence. Now they will go forward to running, climbing and, one day, bike riding. Each and every accomplishment is a stepping stone to the next level.

The ONLY way anyone builds positive self-esteem is by achieving and conquering goals in life, no matter how big or small. It is the only way! By the doing comes the knowing of how it's done. By achieving goals and accomplishments, and by overcoming adversities.

The only way to successfully instill positive self-esteem is for that child or person to acquire it through doing it for themselves in all areas of life and living.

Walk through a fear such as public speaking, monsters under the bed, asking someone to the dance, or telling the truth when knowing you're going to get in trouble for it. When learning any new skill, it holds value in the process.

If you were to teach your child how to drive a car and never let them sit in the driver's seat behind the wheel, they would never understand the mechanics required to operate the vehicle.

All the praise and positive words will not make that happen. A child or person will feel good that someone recognizes their accomplishments, but it will not internally instill a positive self-esteem. Once a person knows they can do something, no one can ever take that away from them. When they know how to change a tire, they do not fear getting a flat. When they know how to spell, they can write whatever is on their mind. When they fear the dark, they can turn the light on and look around.

As a counselor, a woman came to see me over feeling lost and scared of her new life since her husband died. They had been married over 40 years and she had been a housewife the whole time, during which he had done all the bills and maintenance on their home throughout the years.

I questioned her as to, if her husband were alive today, what would she have him do in the house?

She thought it over for awhile and said, "I would like a bookshelf in the family room so I can store all my books in one place."

I told her that I wanted her to buy a bookshelf and assemble it all by herself. Read the directions and take it one step at a time.

She came back the next week all excited to tell me everything she had gone through to make this dream of having her bookcase a reality. Many times she had to walk away from assembling it out of frustration, being at times discouraged, but she stuck with it. In the end, she mastered it and beamed with pride over what she had accomplished. For the first time I could see her self-confidence grow.

I had her do a few more of these homework assignments. With each task, her self-esteem grew, until one day she announced to me that she had come to the conclusion that she could do this now. She would just take each problem and walk through it step by step like a puzzle until it was dealt with. She realized that she could survive life without her husband doing everything for her. I gave her guidance and emotional support along the way, but she did all the work.

The bottom line is that, in the doing, comes the knowing and the gifts. Life is about learning the wisdom to know how, when, where and why to do all things. This never stops as long as we live.

This is true with all things in life. For a parent to do the actions for the child, they could cripple them from learning all aspects of that thing. The child will have built no confidence in them self and will fear it until the day they can master it. Nothing in life is as scary as the unknown. By letting the children walk through it and learn all about that thing... it removes the unknown fears.

Children of parents who enable them while growing up have lifelong difficulties. Have the wisdom to know that, sometimes, the best way to help a struggling child learn is not to do it for them. Let them know you are there for them, help with emotional support, and help guide them as they do the actions themselves.

You as a parent understand how life can be confusing and complicated at times. We do not stop learning and growing, no matter how old we are. Those young years can be filled with how to solve life's puzzles. Teach them the how and the meaning, passion, and purpose will follow. Let them learn what works and what doesn't, because either way, they learn.

PLEASE .... DO NOT DO IT FOR THEM.

Teach Them How
And The
Meaning
Passion
&
Purpose
Will Follow

C.E. Luradel

3

LEARNING

～

There are different levels of learning in our lives. We all begin at birth and learn the basics. Then we get to the intermediate level with academic education at schools. Then we get to advanced levels with relationships and a moral compass for doing life. And last, we reach the highest level, wisdom to know the difference in all life's choices and situations.

We learn things in many ways. For instance, we can observe and learn by example, instruction, or trial and error. Of all these ways, learning by doing keeps the lesson in our memories the longest.

Bottom line, Life is Learning! Every aspect of life and living is learning. Even when discovering how it doesn't work, we learn.

Too much or too little, all or nothing, in most things in life, are equally dysfunctional. Being at the opposite ends of a pendulum, i.e. eating too much or too little, exercising all the time or not at all, working all the time or not at all, lack of praise or over-praising, all have the same effect. Only praise the things that are real. Do not praise just to praise your child a lot. We all know internally if it's real. Be real with your child and praise them when they have truly accomplished something. It could be that they have learned to button up their shirt, or they learned to use three words to make a sentence, or how to apply for a job one day.

The smartest people on our planet do not know everything to recite it at will. What they do know, which makes them smart, is how to find the information that they seek. They know the steps they have to take to access the information. That is a skill that everyone will do well to learn. As human beings, we are not capable of retaining all the information of our world... but with Google, the internet and books, everything is accessible. Show them how, when, where and why, then let go and watch them fly. I call this "earning their own feathers". A bird cannot fly without feathers and neither can a child. Those feathers are required to fly high in life. Each feather represents a skill in their character development that is needed to soar high in life. Feathers that represent learning of such things as honesty, fairness, forgiveness, morals, gratitude, values, love, responsibility, manners, accountability, fear and a positive self-esteem.

You, as a parent, are the best teachers to model how to approach life, to show them how it's done.

Children can be shown that problems are opportunities to learn and grow, and will be viewed as such. Parents model for children that problems in life never stop and how to deal with them. As an adult model for our children, if we present an illusion we have all the answers and no problems, it can set children up to think there is something lacking in themselves. This can lower their self-esteem. Every one of us is a student in life and living, regardless of our age. Parents are teachers; however, they are students as well. When a parent does not know how to handle a situation or problem the first couple of times before they find how it works, this gives the child permission to do so also. The child learns that, because they didn't know the answers the first time, they are not dumb, stupid, or worthless. They will acquire the essential problem solving tools to deal with life's trials and errors.

I view life situations and problems as a puzzle to be solved. That is how life works. Life is full of puzzles just waiting for each of us to solve them.

Failure, for me, is a word that represents I tried. Trying most often results in a failure, until we master the task. We have all tried to walk, talk, sing, or ride a bike, and failed. However, we didn't quit and just kept at it until we got it. So, failure is trying, which is a powerful, empowering action word. Congratulations, you had the courage and strength to try.

One of my first jobs was working for a property management company. I was part of a crew that cleaned up rental homes. Jobs included painting, carpet cleaning, hole patching, yard work, etc., and we were paid by the job – not the hour.

A supervisor accompanied us to each job site. One day, he gave me the task of stripping wallpaper off an 8x10 foot area. Since I had effortlessly performed this task in the past, I thought it would be easy money. In my experience, wallpaper came off in strips. I figured it would take only fifteen minutes of hard work to earn the money for the job.

I started on a corner of the wall, and pulled on the wallpaper. Just a tiny piece pulled off – not the usual large strip! I went to another corner and experienced the same disappointing result. Further tries left me clutching only several tiny bits of wallpaper. Twenty minutes went by, and I was becoming frustrated.

My supervisor watched me working on the wallpaper this whole time and never said a word. Then suddenly, he said, "I'll see you later," and continued his rounds.

Throughout the day, I explored every way I could think of to remove that stubborn wallpaper. I scraped it with a knife, wet it down – and then tried scraping. I picked little pieces off with my fingernails. I even attempted to singe the wallpaper off with a blowtorch the plumber lent me. Occasionally, my supervisor stopped by to watch me work.

Quitting time found me sitting on the floor, glaring at the defaced wall. My supervisor entered the room and sat down next to me. "Have you tried every way you know to strip off the wallpaper?" he asked.

"Yes," I snapped angrily, while looking straight ahead.

"Do you want to know how to remove the wallpaper now?" he questioned.

I whipped my head around to see if he was serious. "Did you know how to get it off the whole time?" I asked in shock.

He grinned, "Yup."

"Well, why didn't you tell me how to remove it this morning, when you saw I was having trouble?!"

"Because you didn't ask. Now, when I tell you how to remove the wallpaper, you won't ever forget it. You exhausted all the possibilities by doing it your way. In the future, you'll be able to handle any wallpaper jobs that come up."

He was right. To this day, I remember how to remove the most stubborn wallpaper. That experience taught me valuable lessons:

1) Even though some things in life worked the first few times that doesn't mean a new aspect won't appear, requiring a different method.

2) New situations may require relearning approaches or behavior we felt we had mastered.

3) I also discovered it is okay to ask for help. Doing so does not mean my intelligence is less than someone else's.

4) Asking for help magnifies the value of the person I ask and makes him or her feel important. They have knowledge I need.

5) If I try something 487 times and fail to get the result I'm after, I still learned 487 other ways. I tried.

6) Do not give up seeking the solution to the problem. For every problem, there is a solution.

7) And most importantly, I learned!

Our society tells us what not to do ... but not what to do. Children look to their parents or caregivers as role models and copy them. Caregivers must model behavior that children can see, hear, feel, and experience. Only then will the child make the connection ... with lasting results.

Parents are not perfect! Caregivers may have grown up in a home with a dysfunctional family unit and may not have learned appropriate or healthy parenting skills. Even those who have had a nurturing and functional upbringing may tell their child to act one way in a situation and defeat that advice by acting in an opposite way. They say one thing and do the opposite.

By facing our learning with a positive mindset, our children will think of adversities, trials, and errors as learning opportunities. There are no mistakes in learning. If I try something ten times, I learn ten ways it does not produce the result I am seeking. However, on the eleventh try, I may find the desired outcome I wanted to achieve. Trying many times does not mean it is bad or wrong. It is learning the ways it does not work – like in the wallpaper example. Therefore, I have learned valuable lessons ... Life is a learning process. We build strength out of the struggles and obstacles in life. Difficulties are opportunities to learn and improve.

There is no such thing as a dumb or stupid person. They are just learning how to do life in all aspects in their own way. Sometimes, it takes multiple ways to solve a problem, and sometimes, it takes only once. Everything is custom made for each one of us.

There is No
Right - Wrong
Good or Bad
Life is
LEARNING
Live it - Grow With it
Enjoy it

C.E. Luradel

Parenting to Prevent and Reverse Problem Behaviors creates a system of learning by doing. I have formulated this system for the whole family. It promotes whole family unit involvement, which can lead to a close bond. Often, I have seen this technique heal the emotional scars of children and parents. It can guide and promote all users toward a more positive direction of life.

As you read this book, use the areas that can work for you and your family. Save other areas for another day if you wish. These methods are flexible and can be modified to your needs. Expand and/or adjust at will. Let your imagination flow.

These methods are esteeming to parents and children. Everyone wants, needs, and deserves to be recognized for their work, values, morals, attempts, accomplishments, responsibilities, dreams, and feelings. These techniques reinforce what we parents have tried to instill in our children for years. When we recognize what they do, they build strong esteem. This allows the child to understand intuitively who they are and where they are going.

This simple system has produced remarkable turnarounds in children considered incorrigible. The *Parenting to Prevent and Reverse Problem Behaviors* program is a powerful tool that can work wonders!

4

CONCEPT OVERVIEW

～

This is a system involving praise and recognition for positive behavior through presentation of Award Certificates. The certificates can be redeemed for items in the family store.

When I started the award system in my family, there were mixed feelings among my children. Some were excited and showed enthusiasm, while one child thought it was ridiculous and did not want to participate. I still went through the steps of explaining how to earn certificates from the Behavior Checklist and how the program worked.

Then, I just waited to see what would happen. My children were my first experiment with the system.

The children who had expressed enthusiasm came home eager to share events of their day and asked if any of their activities earned them Award Certificates. When certificates were issued, the child beamed with pride as the family was told of their behaviors and accomplishments.

Within one week, the reluctant child was won over. She wanted to be part of the family unit praises, too. To date, all my children have become deeply involved with this technique. It has proven to be a joyful and positive family interaction.

Over the years, I have observed patients and others use the Awards Certificate program. Some children take to it right away, while others are reluctant to join in. So far, I have not seen nor heard of any children who did not turn around and become 100% involved.

Allowances

The Award Certificates program is not a program for children's allowance. That is a separate issue that is up to you to continue or not.

Do not use money (cash) as a way of obtaining Award Certificates from the family store. The highest reward is positive emotional acknowledgment, not monetary financial gain.

When a child has a deep desire for something in his or her life, it's called an incentive. Do not eliminate that motivation of the incentive by giving them that item. That would teach them nothing of how life works. A child can use that desire as a motivator to gain knowledge of how to obtain money to purchase that thing they want. Instead, help them brainstorm different ways they could make it happen, such as find materials and turn them into an appealing craft worth selling. Let neighbors know they could mow lawns, wash cars, rake leaves. They need to figure out something outside of doing jobs around the house for their parents.

I heard of a 14 yr old boy who wanted a car when he turned 16, but his parents could not afford one. So, this young man wrote stories and sold them to other kids. He earned over 34 thousand dollars over the next two years. Your child could benefit immensely by learning how to acquire money now, so he or she has that behavior established before entering the adult world with its large financial obligations.

Here is my Cautionary Advice on paying children money to do things around the home: A family is the same as a small business, with everyone working for the betterment of the whole. If a parent pays the child to do things around the house, the child thinks he will be paid to do anything. This sets up a system of the parents doing for the child for free, and the child requiring money in return for what they do.

Parents do many things for their children. Do you require they pay you for doing anything for them? Because a parent pays the child for chores, the child thinks if they do anything for the parent, they need to be compensated for their time and effort. This is a behavior that will continue throughout the child's adulthood. If the child knows and understands they are part of a family unit and all contributions are valued for their participation, it makes the whole family business stronger, healthier, and successful for all.

The Praise Method

This system makes use of the praise acknowledgment method for positive behaviors. The award of certificates and purchase of items reinforces the desired behavior.

The main reason people do things is to receive some kind of payoff. The most rewarding payoff is feeling good about oneself. For instance, when an athlete trains for the Olympics, he or she often works out constantly, day in and day out. Often, these athletes live on a small sum of money and go without luxuries, but their internal force propels them forward. The drive to better themselves is incredible. When that athlete is paid to do the same thing, it becomes a job and the internal self-motivating payoff is missing. Monitory payoffs are not as compelling as internal emotional payoffs. Nothing compares with the strength of feeling good about oneself to promote the repetition of an action. This is where praise comes in.

The act of giving praise becomes just as rewarding for the giver as it does for the receiver. For instance, sometimes, when I look at my baby, I become overwhelmed with love and feel the urge to reach out to hug and kiss her. If I held back, I wouldn't experience the full extent of the love I feel at that time. By holding myself back, I do not get to enjoy the feelings nor do I get joy in return. However, when I act on my feelings, I share my love and enjoy all the sensations of hugging my baby, hearing her giggle, and seeing the pleased look on her face. We both receive the reward. *We get what we give.*

Admittedly, it is easier to criticize than praise. Some parents even discourage praise because they think their job is to point out all the incorrect things. They think the child could do a better job. This does not lend itself to a nurturing and supportive environment. Lack of praise tears down self-esteem, because children do not think they do things right. If you were raised that way, you understand some of the worthlessness it can create within. Full attention to a child's achievement means so much. A smile, a hug, and a few words of congratulations can bring a great deal of satisfaction.

Praise ought to be given right after observing praiseworthy behavior. Small children, especially, need praise following the action. Buttoning his or her sweater is an event to compliment at the time, not when Mom or Dad comes home. Do not tack something onto the compliment like, "Good job... maybe next time you could tie your shoes, too."

Praise can change a child's behavior. One mother was upset about her toddler son hitting the dog. She began praising him for his tenderness when he was gentle and loving to the dog, instead. The boy stopped hitting. Praise is powerful in molding behavior.

One day, my neighbor asked me for advice. She was having behavior problems with her six-year-old son. He was the class bully. She tried many things to turn his behavior around but failed to change his conduct.

I shared the Award Certificate system with her as a possible solution to her dilemma. She took my advice and began the Award Certificate program.

Almost immediately, her son turned around. He would come home from school in an excited state, wanting to share all the things he had done to help his classmates. He helped put books away on shelves too high for some to reach. He gave compliments. He shared classroom toys.

Eventually, instead of wearing an *I-am-bad-and-tough* look, he learned to smile

That was over ten years ago. His mother says he continues the positive behaviors he enthusiastically began with. His classmates and teachers like him for his helpfulness, compassion, and understanding with others. The behavior he was praised for has become a permanent part of his personality.

Life is Full of Puzzles Just Waiting For You to Solve

C.E. Luradel

Family Meetings

An important part of this program is scheduling family meetings once a week. It ought to be a *feel-good* time. Set aside just one hour out of seven days for the family to communicate, brainstorm, laugh, and feel good. It can be a time to promote sharing accomplishments, like school papers or anonymous deeds. Recognize only positives in family meetings – no negatives.

In our home, we chose to open the store after our family meetings. Events we share during the meeting can lead to certificates being given. When we open the store, everyone has his or her awards up to date.

Weekly family meetings can build a family foundation and a tradition that can last a lifetime. It is a wonderful way to pull all age groups together in a common goal and celebration.

If, for whatever reason, a family meeting isn't possible, do your best to let everyone know what amazing behaviors were accomplished this week by each family member.

More Awards Certificate Program Benefits

Children show a lot of enthusiasm about receiving the Award Certificates, because they purchase items from the family store with them. Initially, awards are an incentive for positive behavior but, with time, these positive quality behaviors become a permeate part of their character.

The main objective is to instill values, morals, and responsibility, while building their self-esteem. They learn that, through their positive behaviors, they earn certificates. In that respect, it is an *EARN ALL* program system. A person with a job earns a paycheck. A student attending school earns a grade with hard work and study. Children earn the certificates and learn nothing is handed to them. As in life, if they do not do the work, they receive nothing in return. However, if they do the work to accomplish the task, then they feel good about mastering the job and the getting the praise and reward(s) that come with it.

The items in the family store are items the parents would normally give to their children, anyway. This method encourages children to earn those items, while enhancing their development. People want and need recognition for accomplishments. This system encourages a pat on the back for a job well done. Children cherish praise.

Some children in the family may earn more certificates than others. A child who receives fewer certificates sees her/his sibling(s) being praised and rewarded more. The underachieving child can try to attain more certificates. *The* Awards Certificate system for life & living has further benefits of:

a)   Instilling the concept of saving.

b)   Stopping begging and arguments about wanting to get things.

c)   Establishing realistic values of marketed items.

d)   Building character.

e)   Presenting a clear and concise blueprint of desirable conduct.

f)   Healing emotions.

g)   High value for property purchased using their earned Award Certificates.

h)   Bonding with the family unit, and

i)   Promoting a positive outlook on life … just to name a few things.

A Step-by-Step Overview

1. Establish a family store in the home. A closet is an ideal location, but use whatever you have to work with.

2. Stock the family store with items or pictures of items that are assigned a price tag of what it will cost the buyer. The cost value of each item must be clearly displayed for all to see, such as that item cost is 3, 15, or 70 Award Certificates.

3. The requested Behavior Checklist located in the back of this book must be easily assessable, so all family members can see the behaviors for which they can receive an Award Certificate.

4. Award Certificates are worth a prearranged value – I chose 50¢, but adjust the cost to your own financial situation.

5. Blank Award Certificate forms are not stored in a place that is accessible to all. Any person who is ready to give an award to another family member can complete the form. Children can give Award Certificates to parents or siblings, only with permission from a parent.

6. Once the Award Certificate is filled out and presented to the deserving family member, it cannot be taken away for any reason, with one exception, if they obtained it through dishonesty.

7. The person receiving the Award Certificate can either spend it for items in the family store when the store opens (usually one day a week) or save the certificates for higher-priced items.

8. Family members may also purchase the Buyer \ Seller Family Store Certificates. They can entitle the Buyer to quality time with Mom or Dad, items, or special privileges. Children and adults may sell their services with Family Store Certificates in exchange for Award Certificates.

9. Store hours can be clearly posted on the closet door. I find that once a week for a limited time works well.

10. Most people enjoy keeping their awards certificates as mementos. Therefore, once they are redeemed, they need to be canceled with a stamp or hole punch to indicate they have been spent.

5

FAMILY STORE

❧

Create a location for the family store in your home. What worked best for me was a living room coat closet. Items can be on display and clearly tagged with prices. A second-hand bookshelf works well as a display case. Pictures of items can be displayed. Some of the higher priced items can take over a year (s) to save the required Award Certificates to purchase. The higher priced items are sometimes best displayed using a picture.

The most popular rule is that items cannot be touched – only viewed. If playing with merchandise becomes a problem, the closet can be locked until the store opens (at a set time).

After you decide on the location for the family store, you will need to stock it. Most items that will go into the family store for your child are items you would buy for them, regardless. Now you will just use those everyday items as incentives to teach your children how to do life, while unconsciously building their character. The child will want those items in the store more than they want to do those behaviors listed in the back of this book. However, with time and repetition, these behaviors will become a permanent part of who they are.

Again, remember, obtaining items is an incentive to promote and continue positive behaviors. Please do not stock the family store with items of food, candy, money, or weapons.

Do not use food as a way to obtain Award Certificates, as using food as a way to celebrate or discipline behaviors can set up children for eating disorders. In their future, they will turn to food when things go positive, negative, or both in their life. And do not use money (cash) as a way of obtaining Award Certificates or buying it with Award Certificates from the family store. The highest valued reward is positive emotional acknowledgment, not monetary financial gain.

***

In areas that a child finds difficult, such as math or accepting accountability, you may give double (2) Award Certificates for that behavior being accomplished.

If a behavior comes under the heading of more than one topic on the list, they receive only one Award Certificate for that behavior.

Mid-range and expensive items are included to encourage children to make a goal, plan to reach it, save, and fulfill the goal. Having a long-term goal teaches patience and strategy. The reward is ownership of the item and the self-esteem that follows accomplishment. This is a valuable tool for the foundation of productive adult behavior.

Assigning Prices

I buy items in many price levels (inexpensive, mid-range, and expensive) for our family store. This allows children to purchase weekly, if desired. Adjust the cost value to your budget.

If You buy An Item Anywhere For 1 Dollar Retail	Your Family's Assigned Value For Each Award Certificate Given Out	Amount of Award Certificates it Would Cost to Buy That Item from Your Family Store
1 dollar	1 dollar	1
	50 cents	2
	25 cents	4
	10 cents	10

The examples of cost for items I have listed below are based on my family's 50¢ assigned value rate. One Award Certificate equals 50¢ spent at the retail store for that item. When I buy an item for $1.00, it takes two Award Certificates to purchase that item. I place a sticker on each item in the family store and write a number showing how many Award Certificates it will take to purchase.

If I pay $5.80 at the retail store for an item, it will take 12 Award Certificates to purchase it from the family store. I round it up to the next dollar.

Items costing less than 50¢, I put together as many as it will take to equal the 50¢ value. For example, I put 5 stickers that cost me 10¢ each at the retail store into a bag to equal the 50¢ I paid at the retail store and mark on the sticker price with the number 1 on it.

Overachievers may acquire Award Certificates quickly, so you may have to experiment and modify costs to an affordable level for your budget.

Item Suggestions

The following is a list of item possibilities for a family store. I do not support stocking the family store with candy, food, or weapons as incentives. These suggestions can be tailored to your family's needs and desires.

Inexpensive Items

50¢ to $15 (1 to 30 Award Certificates)

- Stickers
- Rubber stamps
- Various colored ink pads
- Pencils
- Buttons with comical themes
- Hair bands, ribbons, barrettes
- Crayons
- Colored markers
- Felt pens
- Coloring books
- Reading books
- Posters
- Baseball cards
- Trading cards
- Play dough
- Puzzles
- Stuffed animals
- Action figures
- Photo albums
- Framed photographs (taken of friends, pets, etc.)
- Balls
- Favorite music (CDs)
- Favorite sports team merchandise

Mid-range Items

$15 to $30 (31 to 60 Award Certificates)

- Movie DVDs
- Dolls
- Toy cars, trucks
- Board games
- Computer software
- Stuffed animals
- Cameras
- Favorite sports team merchandise

Expensive Items

$30.50 and up (61 + Award Certificates)

- Athletic equipment (football, soccer ball, baseball mitt, surfboard, skateboard, Rollerblades™, etc.)
- Stereo
- TV
- Entertainment unit
- Interactive games
- Computer software
- Bicycle
- Favorite sports team merchandise

Believe me; you will have no trouble stocking your family store. Your children will drop endless hints.

6

BUYER / SELLER FAMILY
STORE CERTIFICATES

∽

Buyer's/Seller Family Store Certificates are documents or printed papers [sample on following page] that can be purchased from the family store with Award Certificates. They entitle the purchaser to the quality time, chore, or privilege written on the certificates. The cost [number of Award Certificates] of each Buyer / Seller Certificates must be clearly written on it.

Children and parents can sell the Buyer / Seller Certificates. Each family member can create a Buyer / Seller Certificate that offers his or her time, talent, labor, or expertise for sale. It is up to the seller to determine the amount of Award Certificates he or she wants to sell the Certificate for.

Family Store Certificate

I _____ certify that the buyer of this certificate will receive:

_____
_____
_____

Date: _____

Purchased By: _____

Due upon the buyer's Discretion of Time and to be established with seller:

COST: _____ Awards

The buyer should be able to receive the stated chore or special time at a period the buyer and seller agree upon. Give sellers a chance to perform their chores in a timely manner.

Purpose of Buyer / Seller Family Store Certificates

It is fun to spend Award Certificates for items from the family store, but it's also rewarding to purchase special time and attention from Mom or Dad, a child's services, or extra privileges.

Parents will be the main buyers and sellers of Buyer / Seller Certificates, because items in the family store will be geared mostly toward the children. This can also be a peaceful way to get chores done around the house. Parents will find it rewarding to realize the value the children place on time and company with Mom or Dad.

The selling of services is a way to:

1. Promote an understanding of the barter system. Children may reduce their pricing on a coupon if they find they have priced themselves out of the market.

2. They learn how to schedule the tasks they are selling.

3. Children can learn the importance of completing a job with care. If they do a good job, they will get repeat sales.

Who Can Sell Family Store Buyer's/Seller Certificates?

Any family member may sell their services with a Buyer / Seller Certificate to any other family member. Again, it is up to the parents whether they want to include other relatives, such as grandparents, aunts, uncles, and so on, in this program.

Buyer / Seller Certificate Suggestions

The following is a list of Buyer / Seller Certificate possibilities. These suggestions may be tailored to your family's needs and desires.

Routine Time/Services

50¢ to $10 (1 to 20 Award Certificates)

- Wash the car

- A ride to and/or from somewhere

- ½ hour - one-on-one time with Mom

- ½ hour - one-on-one time with Dad

- Watch a movie DVD or TV

- ½ hour of time playing board games or cards with _____

- 1 hour of time playing board games or cards with _____

- Perform someone else's cleaning job (rake leaves, wash dishes, take out the trash)

- Stay up late on Friday or Saturday night

- Breakfast in bed

- _____ number of hugs

- ½ hour of driving lessons

Special Time/Services

$10.50 to $20 (21 to 40 Award Certificates)

- 1 hour of driving lessons

- Dinner out with Mom

- Dinner out with Dad

- Double-date with boyfriend/girlfriend (spending money included)

- Date with boyfriend/girlfriend

Deluxe Time/Services

$20.50 and up (41 + Award Certificates)

- Throw a slumber party

- Paint the garage

- _____ [#] of lessons (skiing, ceramics, sketching, painting, horseback riding, guitar playing, martial arts, etc.)

- Summer camp

- Plant a vegetable garden

- Throw a Halloween party

7

AWARD CERTIFICATES

⌒

Award Certificates are documents or printed papers presented to a family member, who performs an action on the Behavior Checklist in the back of the book. When I started, I made the Certificates on MS Word. You can make your own, as I did. Over the years, my Award Certificates have grown to be creative. Samples on the following pages show what they can look like.

Only one Award Certificate may be issued for one behavior on the checklist, such as #21 Reaching a Goal. The certificates can be traded at the family store for items.

It is important to personalize each Award Certificate to bring recognition to the performer and the deed. The person's name is to be written in the top, the date, and the behavior for which the award is being given.

I like to add a few encouraging words. I use red ink, so my comments grab attention. "Fantastic!" "Wonderful!" "Super!" "I'm proud of you!"

These remarks make a person feel special. Sometimes, I add stickers to an Award Certificate. I may also use a rubber stamp with catchwords or animal images.

Award Certificate

To **Chaz**

Date **January 16th**

For **getting an A in reading at school.**

WOW, you read 12 books!!

I'm so proud of you for sticking with it.

Signature

Dad – John Doe

AWARD CERTIFICATE

To **Jill**

Date **March 10th**

For **making personalized signs for gifts**

and selling them for money to help rescue animals.

You are so amazing!!!

Signature

Mom – Jane Doe

Award Certificate

To _Theo_   Date _October 16th_

For _including Joey to play with everyone,_
when he wasn't asked by anyone else.
You're a very special person — thank you for being
thoughtful of others.
I'm glad you're my son :)

Signature
Dad - John Doe

Award Certificate

To _Bohyn_   Date _December 5th_

For _trying to comfort a little girl_
that you didn't even know. I love your big heart...
never stop caring and being who you are!!!

Signature
Mom - Jane Doe

Purpose of Award Certificates

Everyone likes to be recognized for our actions. When my children receive attention for their positive behavior, they beam with pride. My young patients tell me, when their parents praise them, they feel "good," "happy," and "sort of proud."

The effort involved in filling out a certificate and adding little touches means a lot to the recipient. It is an extra pat on the back. Even the act of presentation brings joy to the giver and receiver.

Praise gives a feeling of self-worth and assurance of heading in the right direction. It has the double effect of reinforcing the behavior.

Although verbal praise is welcome, a tangible display lasts and can be saved and reviewed many times. It ought to be up to the recipient whether they want to save their certificates. My children saved theirs in shoeboxes.

Who Can Give Award Certificates?

The whole family can give Award Certificates to each other. It is each family's choice whether they want to include relatives, such as grandparents.

Grandparents Giving to Grandchildren

I had a case where the grandparents wanted to set up their own family store besides the one at the children's home. I advised against it. I felt it would divide the children's efforts to do good deeds because of the differences in the items the two stores would carry. The grandparents could offer better items at greatly discounted prices (spoiling their grandchildren). I urged the grandparents to contribute items to the original family store and keep the original pricing to strengthen the children's sense of value.

Children Giving to Parents

Children can give Award Certificates to their parents. Yes, Mom and Dad receive them, too! Parents become more aware of the examples they set for their children when they are being watched. Remember, children learn through observation. Further, the act of giving an award teaches the skill of praising others for positive conduct.

Siblings Giving to Each Other

Through experience, I have decided that children cannot freely give Award Certificates to each other. They overdo it – to pad the tab – to obtain items from the family store. Each award must be pre-approved by a parent or caregiver.

***

When a child gives an Award Certificate, the act teaches her/him to be aware of the actions of others, and it reinforces positive behavior in the giver.

As the child adjusts to spotting desirable acts, it affects their choice of friends. Children who have used this system choose friends who share their own morals and values. It affects their selection of a spouse and the way they raise their children.

Exceptions to the Award Certificate Technique

Babies and toddlers are too young to participate in this system. Their level of understanding is not developed enough to grasp the idea.

You can include them as soon as you think they can understand some of the basics. For instance, if they put their toys in the toy box, they could receive a certificate and trade it at the store. The earlier the child's positive behavior is reinforced, the better.

Most mentally challenged children also do well on this system. This technique was designed as a simplistic approach that can include almost everyone.

8

WAYS TO EXPRESS PRAISE AND ENCOURAGMENT

❧

As adults, we know how proud we feel when our boss compliments us on a job well done or when our parents gave us words of encouragement. The same goes for our children. They need our approval. It builds their self-esteem and reinforces positive behavior patterns.

For some people, giving praise is difficult. They may not have received encouragement when they were children. It is an important skill to develop at any age.

The following lists suggest ways to express praise and encouragement.

Words of Praise

- Wow
- Superior
- Marvelous
- Impressive
- Remarkable
- Outstanding
- Bravo
- Exciting
- Terrific
- Sensational
- Great
- Beautiful
- Fantastic
- Neat
- Magnificent
- Super
- Spectacular
- Awesome
- Excellent
- Hooray
- Lovely
- Nice
- Wonderful
- Incredible
- Exceptional
- Tremendous
- Phenomenal
- Yes
- Dynamite

Encouraging Phrases

- Super job!
- Nice work!
- You did it!
- I love you.
- I respect your judgment.
- I like being with you.
- You make a difference.
- You got this!
- You are fun.
- You are a good friend.
- You're special.
- Looking good.
- Hooray for you!
- You're important to me.
- I'm glad you were born.
- Thank you for not quitting.
- You really tried.
- You're improving.
- You're beautiful.
- I knew you could do it.
- I trust you.
- You're a winner!
- You're getting it.
- You are important.
- I like you.
- Way to go!
- I'm proud of you.
- You're incredible.
- You're unique.
- Nothing can stop you now.
- Thank you for trying so hard.
- I'm glad you're my son/daughter.

Approving Gestures

- Pat on the back
- Thumbs up
- Approving nod
- Cheer
- Smile
- Jump for joy

- Hug
- Applause
- Wink
- Blow a kiss
- High five
- Give a greeting card

Keep giving praise and encouragement. It means so much to our children.

Life is
LEARNING
the
Wisdom
to Know

How When

Where and Why

C.E Luradel

9

TWO SIDES OF BULLYING

When I was in school there was bullying going on. However, not to the magnitude or cruelty levels of what it is today. At my school, the bullying consisted of being more about exclusion and shunning the kids, such as not letting him play with or including them on a team. Thus, the children who were being snubbed all hung out with each other. There were different levels; the kids that were classified into a social status of being the in-crowd or the losers-crowd.

Years ago, students would classify each other using words such as cool, pretty, handsome, hip, dreamy, and use a rating of 10. And on the other end of that spectrum, they would use words such as nerd, bookworm, four-eyes, geeky, dork, and using the rating of 1 through to 4 as being undesirable.

However, the bullies of today have evolved into groups of children ganging together to take one or more children down. Their words are meant to shatter the child's self-value as a human being to shreds. This gang mentality is reminiscent of what we used to call a lynch mob. A young child has no emotional defense against these brainwashing levels of attacks; even adults would not fare well. The cruelties of the words are so dehumanizing that I will not even list them in this book. The bullies harass on school grounds, before and after school, on the school bus, as well as on social media. Using a well-orchestrated attack strategy, over and over again the attackers tell the child to kill themselves because they are so worthless until that child finally mentally and emotionally breaks down and complies.

My daughter was in sixth grade and the school was having an after-school dance. She was so excited and picked out her best clothes to wear to this memorable event. She had even bought a new white blouse to wear with her black slacks and shoes. That morning, she questioned everyone in the family for their opinion on how she looked. What did they think of her blouse with these pants? Was her hair okay? Did her shoes look alright with these pants? We were unanimous in that she looked beautiful and reassured her she would make some amazing memories of her first dance.

Off she went to catch the school bus up the street out of my view. I knew she would be coming home at 4:10 in the afternoon and I stood in the front picture window watching for her to approach. I wanted her to tell me everything, so we could laugh and smile while she shared the story of her first after-school dance with me.

Finally, the time came and she appeared, walking down the sidewalk with her arms crossed and her head down. I didn't know why, then she looked up and saw me standing there watching her. She burst into tears and ran into the house. I reached for her and asked, "What's the matter, baby? What's wrong? Why are you crying?"

She couldn't talk, she was carrying on so hard, no words could come out and she was having trouble breathing. I just wrapped my arms around her and cried, seeing the emotional pain she was in, and waited until she could speak.

When she was able to speak she told me what happened. While riding home from the dance on the school bus, six boys surrounded her and were saying as many mean insults as they could think of. Insults I cannot and will not put into this book. However, they told her that no would ever want to dance with her and that she was a nauseating maggot, and they would make gagging sounds. They said she was so disgusting that no one would ever want to even touch her, much less dance with her. They even spit all over her new white blouse and hair after each foul name they called her.

My daughter normally had an upbeat personality and found joy in almost everything in life. I always told her that she didn't just think outside the box, she created a whole new container.

I'm fortunate in that my daughter is resilient and, emotionally, she recovered from this bully abuse. Unfortunately, what was supposed to be a happy memory wasn't a happy one, but one she will never forget.

On the flip side is my son. When he was in 2nd grade, he would come home with rips in his shirt. I asked him several times what he was doing at school to keep ripping his shirt and the answer was always the same; playing on the playground equipment or rough-housing with his friends. As time went on, the shirts kept coming home with rips in them and I'd had enough and demanded answers. He confessed that he belonged to a group of kids that were picking on other kids in the playground. I was so shocked that he would have any part in bullying behaviors.

My son was a very loving child and would give a friend everything he owned if they wanted it. He was born with asthma, as well as a club leg & foot that took years of casts & braces to fix. He also had a speech impediment with the letter S, and the sound of TH. In the neighborhood we lived in, he didn't have any friends. The children who lived there saw him as too young and just wanted him to go away. Once, on his birthday, his Grandmother gave him a 20-dollar bill and he spent it all on buying the neighborhood kids candy from the ice-cream man. He was willing to buy their friendship.

He told me that, at school, some other boys had been bullying him ever since 1st grade and, one day, he'd had enough and hit back at one of these boys. He told me it felt good and the other school kids cheered him for having stopped the bully. He smiled when he told me they liked him now and thought he was awesome. I'm a parent that had a child who bullied other kids and I know it isn't easy to see your child in that level of emotional pain and willing to do anything to have friends.

He stopped the bullies and won over the other kids all in one act. Because these other boys thought he was awesome and no one could take him down in a fight, he got the recognition he had always wanted. He found acceptance from these boys in bullying other children, so he and the other boys went around the schoolyard being the tough guys and fighting.

We talked everything out and his bullying days came to an end. I found it so sad that he was willing to do anything just to have a friend.

I'm a parent who has experienced both sides of the bullying and, I can say, both sides brought tears and hurt me. My daughter who never did anything to deserve the cruelty she got and my son snapping and not taking any more and willing to go to any lengths to have a friend. Just writing these horrible incidents out still brings me to tears.

Why Do Children Bully?

For different reasons, such as, they want to fit into a group, they want to show their power over another, to get laughs from likeminded spectators, and they will also use bullying to express their bias-motivated hatred, contempt and/or prejudice against Race, Religion, Gays, Lesbians, Transgender people, or discrimination toward a specific Gender. And sometimes it's because they see in another that part of themselves they hate. Sex, ethnicity, disability, nationality, physical appearance, religion, gender identity; it's an endless list of categories.

On one end of the pendulum, there is a parent that is broken-hearted that their child would ever bully another child, and on the opposite end of that pendulum is a parent defending and promoting their child's right to harm another.

The sad outcome that happens is, one day, a child that had been bullied for years snaps and fights back... and sometimes with devastating outcomes, such as we've all seen in the news of the school shootings. Or the bullied child will believe all the mean and humiliating comments thrown at them and will end it all by taking their own life. The CDC says that over 4,600 children commit suicide each year because of bullying.

Some children/adolescents think it's an easy way to get others to notice them and to be admired for all the wrong reasons. They can also want others to laugh at what they say or do to one another. They think they are a tough guy and that will win friends and help them fit in. By being creative in what they choose to say in a hurtful insulting character-shredding manor that it is funny, they look to win friends. The class clown who needs and wants attention in any way they can get it, even if it means dishing out pain.

There are bullies that are hurting inside so badly that they release their internal hurt onto others by bullying. They will say the words that were said to them at home or elsewhere in their life. You're a freak, dumb, good for nothing, a waste of air, and so on. I have seen those who were bullied who, in turn, will bully as well. They will snap with the emotional pain and harm others, such as we have seen with the school shootings.

However, it's been my personal experience that most who bully grew up being enabled and have huge entitlement issues. They have a false sense of themselves as they've been taught that the world revolves around them. These children grew up in homes where there were no boundaries, limits, or accountability for actions, choices, or behaviors.

As children, they will bully to show their power over others. As an adult, they will bully coworkers, neighbors, cyber-troll people on the internet, and even bully their own spouse.

Warning Signs Your Child Is Being Bullied

Below are some possible warning signs that your child is being bullied. Watch for a continuing pattern of these behaviors, not just a bad day. If your child is NOT being bullied, these signs may indicate some other problem that might need to be addressed.

1. Unexplained black & blue bruises, cuts, scrapes, or marks on their body.

2. Losing property such as toys, school supplies, report card, lunch, or lunch money.

3. Damaged or missing shirt, coat, books, shoes, electronic items, or jewelry.

4. Doesn't want to go to school. Ditch full days or classes.

5. Spends a lot of time in the school nurse's office. Complains of stomach aches and headaches.

6. Afraid of riding on the school bus.

7. Suddenly clingy and afraid to be alone

8. Wants you there waiting for them when school lets out.

9. Change in eating habits, loss of appetite or overeating.

10. Extremely hungry they get home from school. Bullies will take their lunch or money.

11. Becomes withdrawn, evasive, but talks about being lonely.

12. Noticeable sudden changes in normal personality and behaviors.

13. Moody, angry, fearful, and depressed for no apparent cause.

14. Have difficulty sleeping, nightmares, bed-wetting and cries themselves to sleep.

15. Starts bullying siblings or younger children.

16. Waits to use the restroom until they get home.

17. A sudden and significant drop in grades. They cannot focus or concentrate while overwhelmed with fear.

18. Lacks self-esteem. Feelings of not being good enough.

19. Blame themselves for not being good enough in one or more areas.

20. Monitor all electronics for cyber bullying, such as on a cell phone, computer, or tablets. Look for any conflict, particularly controversial, inflammatory remarks, or comments geared to provoking an emotional effect.

21. Talks about wanting to move away; or runs away.

22. Talks about wanting to commit suicide.

Watch your child for what they are not telling you. These behaviors can speak volumes about what might be going on for them. Try to talk to them about possibly being bullied. Let them know you are there for them and together you'll find a solution to this problem. Let them know it's not their fault and they do not deserve to be treated this way, ever. Let them know that it's the bully's way to make them feel bad about themselves and it's all a lie... and please do not believe their words.

If your child insists he isn't being bullied, but you suspect otherwise, arrange to speak with adults who know your child, such as teachers, neighbors, a coach, and other family members. Find out if they think he or she is being bullied and by who, when and/or where. Then please get help for your child.

Warning Signs Your Child Is Bullying Others

I do believe that most parents do not want their child bullying other children. I know that when I found out what my son was doing that I was very emotionally upset.

1. Unexplained black & blue bruises, cuts, scrapes, or marks on their body.
2. Unexplained acquired property such as toys, school supplies, coat, books, shoes, electronic items, jewelry, or money.
3. Unexplained damaged or torn clothing.
4. Noticeable changes in normal personality and behaviors.
5. Starts bullying siblings or younger children.
6. Monitor all electronics for cyber bullying, such as on a cell phone, computer, or tablets. Look for any conflict, particularly controversial, inflammatory remarks, or comments geared to provoking an emotional effect.

School protection for children being bullied needs to be established. Children as young as 7 years old committing suicide is NOT acceptable. Even an 8-year-old committed suicide by hanging himself off his bunk bed because of being bullied. He never told his mother what was going on. Children do not tell because they believe they are what the bully has been told them they are.

PLEASE watch for signs your child is being harmed... or if your child is the one harming others as well. It breaks my heart that there are children out there who are so lost that they find a need to harm others. They need help just as much as the victim does.

Talk to your child about bullying and let them know that you will work out something to protect them that works for both you and your child together. Some kids keep it secret because they fear the bullies will hurt them for telling... or that they would be humiliated in front of the other kids at school. Let them know, whatever the reason, they are safe in coming to you.

Sticks and Stones
Break Bones
But
WORDS
Shred Me to Pieces

C.E. Luradel

10

BEHAVIOR CHECKLIST

⌒

1. **Accepting <u>Accountability</u>**. Admitting the truth to others that you did or did not do something. Being accountable for your own actions, choices, and decisions. Not blaming other people, places, or things for your behavior or making excuses why you did or didn't do it.

   - *"I knocked the lamp over."*

   - *"I did not put the pencils away when I was done using them."*

2. **<u>Achievement</u> in an Extra Activity**. Getting involved in a non-required learning activity in school or outside school. Being involved and participating in a Spelling Bee, Sport, Music, Art, Dance, Cheerleading, Choir, Acting, Journalism, Political Elections, 4H Club, completing an elective school project, or anything you learn outside of the required academics classes in school.

3. **<u>Apologizing</u>**. When you realize your behavior is not okay and it has hurt or may have hurt someone else, you apologize. When you have harmed or hurt another, apologize, unless to do so will cause harm to another or yourself. Also, apologizing for not following the rules in life, school, home, or work.

    -   *"Michael, I'm sorry for the mean things I said yesterday."*
    -   *"Mom, I'm sorry I didn't clean up my mess, even when I knew I had to do it."*
    -   *I'm sorry, Mr. Todd. I didn't share the paper with Dean."*
    -   *"William, I'm so sorry I accidently pushed you out of the way when I was running to the cafeteria table."*

4. **<u>Appreciation</u>.** Expressing and/or displaying gratitude for something someone has done. Acknowledging what that person did. Thanking them directly and/or praising them to others for what they did.

- *"Thank you, Robert, for helping me with my homework."*

- *"Hey Jill, Kaylie did an awesome job helping me yesterday with my homework."*

- *"I wrote a thank you for all the help Willow did for me on my Facebook page for all my friends to see."*

- *"I wrote Donnie a thank you note for helping me with my homework and gave it to him at school today."*

- *"I placed a video I recorded on the internet of a woman saving a dog from getting hit by a car. She was awesome; she saved him."*

5. **Asking**. When you ask someone if you can or cannot do something. Asking to touch, borrow, use, or have something.

  - *"Jody, can I please borrow your basketball to play with my friends out front for a while?"*

  - *"Ann, can I play with your dollhouse, please?"*

6. **Receiving a School, Award**. Receiving an award for behavior, grades, participation, performance etc.

7. **Courteous Borrowing**. When you quickly return an item you have borrowed. If the item becomes damaged while in your care, you either repair or replace it and apologize. You take responsibility for another person's property.

  - *"Here's the book I borrowed last week for my homework. I kept it clean."*

8. **Honoring <u>Commitments</u>**. When you promise, or give your word that you will or will not do something.

    - *"I promised I would be there at 4:00. I gave my word. I was there at 4:00."*

    - *"I said I wouldn't call anyone 'stupid' anymore. I don't even speak the word anymore."*

9. **Complimenting**. Telling another person you like a certain thing about her or him. You give a compliment when you mean it.

    - *"Chaz, you did a good job throwing that ball to Bradlee." (b) "Felicia, I like your dress."*

    - *"Mom, this meal tastes delicious."*

10. **<u>Complimenting</u> People You Do Not Like**. Find something, anything, you like about that person. Something that you like and admire. It is a nice thing you say to their face or say to another person about them. You must mean it.

    - *"Ryan, you really played a good soccer game this season." You can pass along a compliment by telling someone your thoughts. If you are talking to Jill, you could say,*

    - *"I think Ryan played a great game of soccer this season."*

11. **Being Aware of Consequences**. Becoming aware that, when you did something, the outcome was positive (what you want - desired result) or negative (what you do not want - undesired result). Thinking of a different way to do it.

   ▪ *"I didn't wear my gloves when I went outside to play today. My hands were so cold it hurt. From now on, I will always wear my gloves when I go out to play in the snow."*

   ▪ *"Today, I helped Willow carry some boxes to the library. She smiled at me and said I was a great help. It felt good inside, and I like that good feeling that came from helping people."*

12. **Receptive to Constructive Criticism / Critique**. Calmly listening to someone who confronts you with a behavior of yours that they do not like. Then, replying to them, "Thank you for sharing that with me." Think it over for a day and decide if it is true. If you feel they have a point, you work on changing the behavior.

   ▪ *Someone: "I don't like the way you chew your food with your mouth open. I can see the food and hear you crunching it." You: "Thank you for sharing that with me." One day later, you decide to chew your food with your mouth closed. You work on remembering to do so when you eat.*

13. **Performing Helping <u>Deeds</u> or <u>Services</u>**. Performing an act of kindness for someone (family member, friend, acquaintance, stranger, neighbor, etc.) you think would be appropriate for his\her needs or wants. This can be planned

   - *"I'll walk your dog for you, Mr. Todd." or unplanned. You see the elderly Mrs. Ellen trying to lift her grocery bags from the car.*

   - *"Let me help you carry in those groceries for you, Mrs. Ellen."*

14. **Secretly Performing Kind <u>Deeds</u> or <u>Services</u>**. Anonymously doing something kind for someone you think would be appropriate for her/his needs or wants. This can be planned or unplanned. To perform this deed successfully (#14), no one's to know who did it, except your family. If the person knows you did it for her/him, it becomes #13.

   - *Leave a note in a new student's desk, telling her/him you are glad she/he is in your class and do not sign your name. Let them think everyone in the classroom is the person who left the note, and they will feel even more welcome.*

   - *Mail selected food coupons to someone who uses those items or leave them at a neighbor's door. You may also place them in the store, by the items advertised, for a stranger to use.*

- *Write a letter to someone that says you are glad they were born or another sentiment they may need to hear.*

- *Draw a picture for your teacher that includes appreciation for his/her hard work.*

- *Leave flowers on someone's desk or by their door, with a note stating they deserve flowers.*

15. **Empathizing**. When you understand and share the emotional feelings of another. You either know how it feels or you can imagine how it would feel if it happened to you. Then, you either do something about it or acknowledge his/her feelings.

    - *When you watch someone crying on TV and you cry too, because you feel sad for what happened to him or her.*

    - *When a student is called a name, you feel sad and angry about what happened to them.*

    - *You feel happy for a student who won a race because you see and feel his/her joy.*

16. <u>**Fail.**</u> There is no such thing as you, as a person, failing … it's trying to do something that didn't work. If I do not try, I will never know what works or doesn't work for "Me". If you try and it didn't work, then congratulations; you tried. The more you fail, the more you are trying.

- *"Today, I tried to jump the double rope really fast, but I kept falling down."*

- *"I tried to color a picture using water colors and the paint ran together, making one color. It didn't work out so well."*

- *I tried to throw the ball through the basketball hoop, but I wasn't strong enough to make it that high."*

- *I tried to tie my shoe laces, but I just don't get it."*

- *I tried to give Rylie my apple at lunch today, but she wouldn't take it."*

17. **Appropriately Expressing <u>Feelings</u>**. Identifying and appropriately expressing your feelings. Not hurting people or property when expressing your strong feelings of anger, loneliness, sadness, fear, pain, or guilt.

   - *Crying when you are sad and admitting you feel unhappy to someone who is safe to talk to.*

   - *Being angry - walk it off, or writing it all out.*

   - *Being lonely - go to where the people are and join in.*

   - *Being scared - talk about it with someone you trust.*

   - *Feeling guilty for something you did or didn't do – apologize - change it - and never do it again.*

18. **Forgiving**. To forgive someone who wronged you. Forgiving others is necessary for personal growth. Forgiveness frees up your mind and heart to find other things in life to smile about. Forgiveness is a gift you give to yourself. Forgiveness is letting go of grudges and bitterness. Resentments of anger and revenge will overwhelm your thoughts, life, and your happiness. Even forgiving people who are not accountable for anything they have done or have not done. Not holding a grudge. Also, accepting an apology from others who hurt you.

   - *When I forgave Michael for hurting my feelings, I could concentrate on my book report and smile with my friends over silly, funny things again."*

   - *"When Dean told me he was sorry, I told him I accept his apology and hope we could continue to be friends."*

19. <u>**Goal**</u> **Action Plan**. Design a plan for achieving a selected goal. Map out the steps of what you need to do to make your goal vision become a reality.

   - *"I have decided I'm going to try out for the football team next year. I'm going to watch videos and read play books on how to play football like the pros every weekend to get better at it."*

   - *"I want to get along better with my sister. First, I will listen to what she says without correcting her on where she is wrong. And second, unless she asks, I won't tell her how to do things and let her learn how on her own."*

20. **List of Lifetime <u>Goals</u> you want to achieve.** Make a blueprint for your life. List all the things you want to accomplish. List all the specific goals and any plans of accomplishing those goals. How and by when. *(Meet the Pope by 2034, visit France in the spring, write a book on how to get what you want, paint a picture on canvas using oils, find a cure for cancer, go to college and get a PhD in chemistry, fly an airplane before I'm thirty, sail around the world in a boat, learn a different language before age 60.)*

21. **Reaching a <u>Goal</u>.** You achieved a planned goal. You made it happen.

- *"I made the football team!"*
- *"I finished writing my book!"*

22. **Earning Outstanding <u>Grades</u>.** Earning an A or B on a test or report card.

23. **3 Things You Feel <u>Gratitude</u> About.** Having gratitude means you're thankful for what something or someone did or something you're grateful you experienced that day. Notice the gifts each day gives to you. Be happy you saw, heard, or felt something that you are glad happened. A sunrise, sunset, flowers, music, laughter, sadness that taught you something. Make a list of at least 3 things in a day you are grateful that happened in your life and in your world.

- *"Grayce and I looked into flowers at their designs and how pretty and different each one is."*

- *"I saw a puppy and a kitten wrestling around together and it made me laugh."*

- *"Today, I watched Bohyn give a speech in the auditorium, and I felt proud he is my bother."*

- *"It rained today, and I had so much fun playing in the mud with Ryan. I'm so glad he is my friend."*

- *"In school today, there was a picture of a bunch of kids that have no shoes to wear because they are too poor. I realized I'm rich because I have 4 pair of shoes and money to buy even more."*

- *"Donnie was walking around the room like a chicken, and it made me laugh."*

24. **Being <u>Honest</u> under Pressure**. When telling the truth may get you or someone else in trouble, but you tell the truth, anyway. It's easy to tell the truth when there is no pressure of getting into trouble, but to do so even when you know you might get negative consequences shows you are a person with a high integrity and ethics level.

- *"Jake told me he'd beat me and my sister up if I told, but he's making me give him my lunch money every day."*

- *"Yes, it was me who took the glass of water out front and left it there."*

25. **Including People who are Excluded**. Noticing that a person has been left out of something and trying to correct it.

    - *You notice Robert wasn't asked to go to the playground to play with the other kids. You say, "Hey, Robert, come and play with us."*

26. **Listening Attentively**. When someone talks to you, you listen to what they say, without interrupting. You do not change the subject or interject with talk about yourself. You maintain eye contact, face the speaker, and keep your body still.

27. **Love.** Is the most powerful and universal emotion known. We ALL want to love and be loved. Such a small word can invoke a wide range of intense emotional reactions. Love is feeling emotion when using any of our 5 senses, which activates an internal experience. The effects of love are Compassion, Empathy, Joy, Happiness, and yes, even in Sadness. Compassion is caring what happens to another. Empathy is when one feels the emotional experience of another. The same is true when we feel Sad when we emotionally experience the pain and suffering of another. Joy is being happy

because of a positive pleasant action, thing, or experience. Happiness is an internal feeling of peace and contentment. There are many types of love: the love of a Parent for their child, the love of a dog for his owner, the love a person feels in a romantic relationship, and the love for a close friend. Love can be for people you know or for complete strangers, animals, nature, art, music, talent, or creativeness.

- *"When I climbed the ropes today in school everyone cheered me on, I felt loved.*

- *When I heard Gracy play her violin, it was so relaxing that it took me to a peaceful place inside of me. I fell in love with her talent.*

- *I saw a man give his shoes to someone who didn't have any; I felt such deep compassion for both of them.*

- *It felt so peaceful watching the sunrise grow brighter as it got higher in the sky.*

- *I saw how much the dog loved the homeless man, even though he didn't have anything for him.*

- *It made me cry and love Mrs. Ruth when I found out she cut back on her food so she could send her grandson a birthday card with five dollars in it.*

- *I found a note on my desk in school today telling me they were glad I was in their class. I felt so wanted that my eyes started to water.*

- *Today, we found Clair's blind dog that was lost in the woods. I'm so happy I can't stop smiling.*

- *The fireman rescued the deer that fell through the ice. I'm so happy she was saved.*

- *I saw my 22-month-old younger brother walk over to a little girl that was crying, squat down, rub her arm like Mom does, and give her his cookie, trying to help her feel better. I was so proud he was my bother that I almost cried.*

- *At school, some bullies circled a girl and were saying awful mean things to her. She was crying, asking them to stop, and they would not. All I could do was cry for her because she was hurting so bad."*

28. **Being Loyal**. Being a true friend.

   - *You do not drop a friend for the friendship of someone else.*

   - *You do not talk negatively about another person, nor do you listen to faultfinding gossip.*

29. **Using Manners**. You use proper manners.

   - *You say, "Please," "Thank you," and "Excuse me."*

- *You eat with your mouth closed, don't burp in front of others, do not curse, and use napkins when you eat.*

30. **<u>Modeling</u> Healthy Appropriate Behavior**. Showing by doing. Modeling healthy and appropriate behaviors by being an example of how it is done.

    - *William sees Ellen telling the truth, even when she could get into trouble for it. He admires her courage & strength and wants to do that too.*

    - *Jill picked Ryan to be on her team when others would not. All the other kids noticed she was a fair and loving person at heart.*

    - *Dad sees Dean spill his milk because he wasn't paying attention when he reached for it on the kitchen table. Instead of getting angry and yelling, Dad says, "Accidents will happen, Dean. Just hurry and clean it up please, so we can go to Grandma's house."*

31. **Ability to Show Knowledge a <u>Need</u> versus a <u>Want</u>**. Knowing what a need is versus a want. Tell what the difference is when you desire something. Give verbal examples of each.

    - *Needs: bed, food, and shoes. Wants: waterbed, cotton candy, and $100 designer sneakers.*

32. **Noticing the <u>Needs of Others</u>**. Listening when someone talks about what he/she needs or noticing someone has a need.

   - *"I noticed José didn't have any lunch at school today, so I shared mine with him.*

33. **Developing a Positive <u>Outlook</u>**. Finding a positive in something you thought was a negative… and you find value. This is called reframing your thinking.

   - *"My sister kept knocking on the door while I was talking with my Mom. At first, I got mad, and then I realized she just loved and missed me because I'd been gone overseas for over a year."*

   - *"I was seated with people I didn't know. I was upset because I wanted to sit with my friends, whom I knew. I noticed a girl sitting next to me was drawing some good-looking pictures in a notebook. I started a conversation by telling her I thought she could draw well. We talked a lot about art, and now, I'm so glad I was made to sit next to her and we got to meet. I gained a new friend."*

   - *"I didn't want to work in a group for my school project assignment. I have great writing skills and can do it myself, in my own way. Then I realized Willow can draw so well that she could do the visual arts aspects easily. And Jody knows how to create an outstanding presentation much better than I can.*

I realized each person in our group was strong in their own way, and because of it, we made our assignment even that much greater."

34. **Best Question you asked your Teacher Today?** Because you are actively listening to what is being taught, you know what question to ask to learn more about that subject... and you ask that question and learned the answer.

35. **Not <u>Quitting</u>**. When you don't quit – no matter what happens – and accomplish the goal. Turn "I want to give up!" into "I did it!" When it doesn't work the first time or even after several tries, you hang in there. This applies to a goal, job, behavior, school, relationship, and problems.

   - *"I kept trying to get over that hurdle on the track, and I just kept hitting the top and falling down. My coach told me I needed to work on building my muscles using weights to make my legs stronger to left me higher. It Worked! I made it over the hurdles last week. I'm so glad I didn't quit."*

   - *"I wanted to write that book, but I didn't think I could do it. I was told to write for one hour a day, and wow, I got it done."* (c) *I watched Bohyn trying to ride his bike, and he just couldn't get it. He kept trying over and over again. Even though he got frustrated each time he fell, he just kept getting back on and working at getting it. He never quit and then, he got it!"*

36. **Working on Self-Improvement**. Learning how to improve yourself through education. Reading a book, listening to tapes, and attending classes or lectures on self-improvement of mind, body, or spirit.

37. **Being a Self-Starter**. When you perform your tasks without being asked or reminded to do so.

    - *You set your clock to get up on time all by yourself. (b) You remember to do your chores without someone asking you to do them.*

    - *You set aside time for homework and studying all on your own.*

38. **Sharing Time, Possessions, or Space.** Taking turns with time or possessions. Honoring another person's personal Time.

    - *"I wanted Dad spending time with me, not my sister. Then I realized it was her turn, so I found something else I could do while they talked."*

    - *"We had to sit on the same seat together, and I didn't want to, but I decided to share the chair and not fight about it."*

    - *"I watched Jocelyn handing out strawberries to all her friends today. She wanted everyone to have some, not just her."*

39. Demonstrating Positive <u>Sportsmanship</u>.

- *Being a kind and fair winner or loser. This means not making fun of the losers when you win or throwing a tantrum when you lose.*

- *Letting other people play their way, without trying to control how, when, where, or who plays.*

- *Not cheating or making up rules that give you a better chance of winning.*

- *Cheering on your opponent to succeed. Letting them know you think they can do it.*

- *Complimenting the other players when the game has ended. (f) Praising the other player who won, letting them know you think they did an awesome job winning the game.*

40. We Are The <u>World Service</u>. Helping To Make Our World A Better Place For Everyone. Formulating ways to help our world be better place for everyone. Formulate a plan and make it happen.

- *Organize how to find bottles to cash in for the money to donate to animal rescue organizations.*

- *Foster care home for a rescued animal*

- *Carry groceries home for the elderly*

- *Make items out of pine cones lying in the forest on the ground. Sell them to get the money to buy homeless people socks, shoes, or coats.*

Resolution Chairs

This is an Opportunity For Learning

How to Obtain Resolution

When Children get into an Argument

1. Sit each arguing child into chairs that are pulled together. Side by side or facing each other.

2. The children are to remain in their chair until each child can tell you what THEIR part was in this argument.

3. If only one child can say what they did, and the other(s) can not, all continue sitting on the chairs until everyone can say what THEIR part was in this argument.

4. After they all tell you what their part was in this argument, they must now tell you what they could do differently if this were ever happen again.

5. Lastly, each child apologizes to the other(s) for their behavior in this argument.

INVITATION TO READERS

∽

Parenting doesn't come with a manual, and as parents we've all had our difficulties along the way. I would love to hear all about your journey using this method of Parenting as your Manual. By sharing your story, another family or parent with the same problem could benefit from knowing they are not alone in their journey. I look forward to reading all your emails and I Thank You for sharing.

***

Most of my Family Store & Award Certificates were created in full color. If you would be interested in purchasing a set of these Certificates for your own family, please send me your email address with Certificates written in the subject line. If I receive enough interest from people wanting them, I will notify you if & when they become available.

C. E. Luradel
luradel@gmail.com